a reason for

Handwriting

Teacher Guidebook

Cursive

ISBN #0-936785-49-7

Published by Concerned Communications
700 East Granite • P.O. Box 1000 • Siloam Springs, AR 72761

Authors **Carol Ann Retzer, Eva Hoshino**
Publisher **Russ L. Potter, II**
Senior Editor **Bill Morelan**
Creative Director **Daniel Potter**
Copy Editor **Tricia Schnell Williams**
Proofreader **Trish Houston**
Illustrations **Rob Harrell**
Colorists **Josh & Aimee Ray**

Copyright ©2001 by **The Concerned Group, Inc.**
All national and international rights reserved. Except for brief quotations in reviews,
no part of this publication may be stored or transmitted in any form, or reproduced
by any means (photocopy, electronic, mechanical, recording, etc.).

Scripture translation selected for appropriate vocabulary level.
All verses are taken from *The Living Bible*, Tyndale House Publishers,
Wheaton, Illinois 60187. Used by permission.

printed on recycled paper

For more information about **A Reason For**® curricula,
write to the address above, call, or visit our website.

www.areasonfor.com
501.549.9000

A Personal Message from the Authors of

A reason for Handwriting

Dear Friends:

It seems like only yesterday. Recess had just ended, and as the children took out their pencils and paper, I began writing the day's handwriting lesson on the blackboard: "Only one cow, Clarabell, came."

Suddenly I stopped. How many hours had my students spent focusing on such meaningless sentences? Impulsively I erased the board, then wrote "Our God is so good!"

And from that humble beginning back in 1979, came **A Reason For® Handwriting**—the K-6 Scripture-based handwriting curriculum now used in thousands of private and parochial schools nationwide!

A Reason For® Handwriting was developed with three basic goals in mind. First, to help children develop proper handwriting skills. Second, to incorporate Scripture verses designed to inspire young hearts and minds. And third, to help children experience the fun and fulfillment of sharing God's Word with others.

In short, **A Reason For® Handwriting** helps integrate faith and learning to bring students closer to Christ. And after all, isn't that what our schools are all about?

May God richly bless as you continue to touch young lives for Him!

Carol Ann Retzer & Eva Hoshino
A Reason For® Handwriting

Table of Contents

General Guidelines for
Teaching Cursive

Handwriting is an essential skill for children and adults alike. Even in today's high-tech world, it's a skill we use every day!

And legible handwriting is a critical skill in the classroom, too. High school and college students increasingly feel the need for quality handwriting as they face the essays required on many of today's standardized tests.

Unfortunately, there are no shortcuts in learning to write legibly. It does not occur automatically with age maturity, but is a learned motor skill that requires constant practice! And yet, "perfect" handwriting should never be an end in itself. Ultimately, the focus should be on the *message* rather than the process.

A Reason For Handwriting provides the ideal message for your students to focus on — God's Word! In short, since success is achieved only by consistent, daily practice, why not focus that practice on the values found in Scripture verses?

The Teacher's Role

In most schools, students are introduced to cursive letter formation in the second or third grade. But this doesn't mean further handwriting instruction is unnecessary. Handwriting workbooks don't teach handwriting—TEACHERS do! Simply put, the process of learning legible handwriting is greatly enhanced by continued monitoring and guidance from an informed teacher.

Because children tend to imitate the teacher in their handwriting, you should become thoroughly familiar with all the letter forms used in *A Reason For* Handwriting in order to demonstrate the individual letter strokes correctly. Even though it's similar to many traditional methods, *A Reason For* Handwriting is a unique handwriting style. Please take a few moments to review both the Cursive and Manuscript Letter Formation Charts (see Appendix, page 80).

The Weekly Schedule

A Reason For Handwriting should be part of your daily classroom schedule. Each section is designed to take 10 to 15 minutes to complete, since longer periods cause many children to tire and lose efficiency. Most students quickly grasp the simple weekly format, allowing them to focus their attention on the lesson tips, applications, and daily practice.

A great time to teach *A Reason For* **Handwriting** is immediately after opening exercises. The program's Scripture-based content makes it ideal for beginning the day! And when you *begin* with handwriting, you can draw students' attention to practice letters throughout the school day.

Remember, it's counter-productive to let your students complete an entire week's lesson in one sitting! Only regular *daily* practice can bring effective results. The key is the *quality* of the practice, not the quantity!

Alternative Methods & Remediation

Many students are not visual learners, and need more than just a model to help them effectively improve their handwriting.

To maximize their learning experience, be sure to include some of the recommended alternatives (verbal description, board practice, sky-writing, etc.) to demonstrate both letter size and formation. Board practice in small groups is especially helpful. It not only reinforces student learning, but also makes it easier to spot letter formation problems of individual students.

If students are having problems with certain letter groups, suggest that they practice sections of the "Letter Group Charts" (Appendix, page 82). If students have difficulty with a specific letter, suggest they practice writing the letter in groups of three (see "Connecting Stroke Practice," Appendix, page 89). It's really amazing how quickly a student's handwriting will improve when a specific area is remediated!

Evaluation & Motivation

Letting students know exactly what's expected is always helpful—especially when it comes to legible handwriting! As students are made aware of the evaluation system (see "Tips on Grading," page 7 and "Be a Five Star Student," Student Workbook, page 6), their work will improve remarkably. The evaluation system also provides a reference point to pinpoint specific areas (alignment, slant, size, shape, and spacing), and facilitates parent/teacher interaction. Scripture Border Sheets are also a powerful component of

A Reason For Handwriting. When students know that their handwriting will be shared with others (see "Ways to Share," page 8), they're motivated to do their *very best* work. You may assign specific border sheets each week, or let students select their own. (Note: Several border sheets feature holiday themes. Have students save these until the appropriate time.) Sharing Scripture Border Sheets can generate positive community interaction, and creates good will for your school!

Scripture Translation

Since *A Reason For* Handwriting was designed to teach elementary handwriting, using a Scripture translation with simple, easy-to-understand vocabulary was essential. Each Verse of the Week used in this series is taken from *The Living Bible* by Tyndale House Publishers.

Weekly
Lesson Format

The pattern of daily lessons in *A Reason For* Handwriting repeats from week to week. This format minimizes the time needed each day for verbal instruction, and maximizes your students' time on task. Specific lesson tips, answers to discussion questions, and extended teaching suggestions for each lesson are found in the **Daily Lesson Plans** section, beginning on page 12.

Here is the suggested weekly lesson format:

Day One

Read the Verse of the Week together. Discuss the daily lesson tip. Point out the focus letters or words for the day.

Day Two

Read the Verse of the Week together. Review the focus letters or words for the day. Use the extended teaching tips as time permits.

Day Three

Same as Day 2.

Day Four

Read the Verse of the Week together. Have students practice the entire verse once or twice on a sheet of paper. Ask the students to select a Scripture Border Sheet from the back of their workbooks and begin decorating it.

Day Five

Challenge students to repeat the Verse of the Week from memory. Have students carefully write the Verse of the Week on their chosen Scripture Border Sheet, then finish decorating it. Discuss ways students can share their finished Scripture verses. (See page 8 for ideas.)

Tips on
Grading

Grading System

There are five basic areas the teacher should consider when evaluating handwriting form. They are alignment, slant, size, shape, and spacing. The "Be a Five Star Student" section in the Student Workbook (page 6) has detailed descriptions of each area, and is designed to help you reinforce the evaluation process. Allowing 2 points for each item results in an easy-to-understand 10 point grading scale (see Appendix, page 93). If this system is used regularly, it helps students and parents understand how the final grade will be determined.

General Guidelines

It is important to keep handwriting evaluation as positive as possible. Look for the students' *best* work! Also, emphasize consistent writing from day to day, and focus on the *quality* of the student's handwriting rather than just quantity.

Student Folders

It's a good idea to keep a folder for each student with samples of his/her work. This should include pages from the beginning and ending of each grading period (either the alphabet or Day 4 practice). Thus, when grading time arrives, evaluation can be based on each individual student's progress.

Evaluation Sentence

The practice sentence at the bottom of the page (also see Student Workbook, page 6) contains all the letters of the alphabet. Ask students to write this sentence at the beginning of the grading period — then again at the end. Comparing the two will help you pinpoint specific letter problems.

This sentence may also be used for one minute timed writings. While speed is not the primary concern in handwriting, some students may benefit from this practice. Be sure to encourage readability as well as speed!

The following practice sentence contains all the letters of the alphabet:

God created the zebras and foxes to walk, jump, and hide very quickly.

Ways to Share

An exciting part of *A Reason For* Handwriting is the opportunity students have for sharing God's Word with others. While students enjoy writing and decorating the Verse of the Week, the real excitement begins when they *share* the finished Scripture Border Sheet with others.

● Place the verse in a spot where members of the family will see it every day.

● Make a placemat! Center the sheet on construction paper or a plain paper placemat. Laminate or cover with clear contact paper.

● Find someone who is housebound. Deliver the verse in person, and stay to visit.

● Give the decorated verse to grandparents. Don't forget a personal note — either on the back, or on a page of practice paper.

● Share the verse with someone who works at school: the secretary, custodian, principal, or even board members!

● Encourage other Christians. The church secretary can often provide names of those who'd appreciate a Scripture verse of encouragement.

● Take a trip to a nursing home. Have a pair of students visit each resident, then leave their verses to decorate the room.

● Give the verse to someone who is sick. Some hospitals will cooperate by placing the verses on patients' breakfast trays.

● Create an attractive bulletin board using the Scripture Border Sheets. Or select a special one each week, and display it in a special place in your classroom.

● If the school has a central display case, ask permission to periodically post a Scripture Border Sheet from the class.

● Check to see if your church would like to display the verses, or enclose one with each copy of the church newsletter.

● Ask for a church mailing list. Send each family a Scripture Border Sheet and a personal note. Do a few each week. Students will be delighted with the positive response this will generate!

Suggested Cover Letter

People receiving the verses are often more responsive when a letter that describes the sharing program is included. Writing this letter on your school letterhead adds a nice touch. Here's a sample you can use:

Dear Friend,

Each week our class writes a Scripture verse as part of our handwriting lesson. This week we want to share a verse with you.

We hope you have a good week with God's blessing. We will be praying for you.

Sincerely,

(Your name)

Proper Positioning

Paper Position

Right- and left-handed students should learn the same principle of paper placement. Students should place their paper at the same angle as the arm they use for writing (see illustrations). Demonstrate how the page can easily be moved up as the writing nears the bottom of the page. (Note: These paper positioning principles apply to both cursive and manuscript writing.)

Special attention should be given to left-handed students. Correct paper placement (see above) and pencil position will help the student write without a "hooked hand" position, or an exaggerated head tilt.

Body Position

A good writing position provides comfort and balance. Encourage the students to:

- Sit comfortably back in the seat, facing the desk squarely.

- Place both feet flat on the floor.

- Lean slightly forward, but without letting the body touch the edge of the desk.

- Rest both forearms on the desk.

- Hold the paper in place with the free hand.

Pencil Position

The student should hold the pencil between the thumb and index finger, letting it rest lightly on the middle finger. The thumb should be about half an inch above the sharpened part of the pencil.

Please Read This First!

Before you begin the daily lessons, please make certain your students clearly understand the following:

The mechanics of handwriting (see **Proper Positioning**, page 9).
The format of the class (see **Weekly Lesson Format**, page 6).
The evaluation process (see **Tips on Grading**, page 7).

It's also very important to have each student write the alphabet (capital and lowercase letters) on a sheet of paper, then sign his or her name and date it. You'll use this sheet later to pinpoint areas of special need, either for individual students, or for the entire class. It's also a good plan to keep this sheet on file to aid in evaluation for the next grading period.

Most importantly, remember that as you acknowledge and reward progress, the learning process is greatly enhanced!

Daily Lessons

Scripture Verse

"Love forgets mistakes; nagging about them parts the best of friends. A true friend is always loyal, and a brother is born to help in time of need." Proverbs 17:9, 17

Tip of the Week

"A good goal for this year is to improve your handwriting as you share God's Word with others. Review the **Five Star** evaluation (Student Workbook, page 6) with your teacher to see how you measure up."

Letter Focus

A a, U u, N n

NOTE:

Directions must be used as part of the Weekly Lesson Format. See page 6.

Lesson 1

TIP OF THE WEEK

A good goal for this year is to improve your handwriting as you share God's Word with others. Review the **Five Star** evaluation (page 6) with your teacher to see how you measure up.

Day One Practice the following letters and words from this week's Scripture.

A a
about
loyal
always

Day Two Continue practicing letters and words from this week's Scripture.

U u
true
born
brother

9

Copyright©2001 by Concerned Communications. All rights reserved.

Extended Teaching

• Review the **Five Star** evaluation with your students (see page 7). Explain your grading procedure and encourage students to set personal goals within these five areas.

• File a sample of each student's writing to serve as a starting point for future evaluation. Use either this week's Day Four practice — or have students write the complete alphabet (capital and lowercase). Be sure to date the sample.

For Discussion

"List the characteristics of a good friend." (loyal, trustworthy, supportive, etc.) "What things on this list describe you?" (Answers will vary.) "How could you be a better friend?" (Notice when classmates are happy or sad, say kind words to classmates, etc.)

Day Three Continue practicing letters and words from this week's Scripture.

Nn

need

friend

nagging

Day Four Write this week's Scripture verse on a sheet of practice paper.

Love forgets mistakes; nagging about them parts the best of friends. A true friend is always loyal, and a brother is born to help in time of need.

Proverbs 17:9,17

FOR DISCUSSION

List the characteristics of a good friend.
What things on this list describe you?
How can you be a better friend?

10

Copyright©2001 by Concerned Communications. All rights reserved.

Lesson 2

✏ Scripture Verse

"Despise God's Word and find yourself in trouble. Obey it and succeed. The advice of a wise man reflects like water from a mountain spring." Proverbs 13:13, 14

✏ Tip of the Week

"Make certain your lowercase *e*'s and *i*'s are easily distinguishable. Poorly written, these two letters account for many spelling errors."

✏ Letter Focus

Dd, Gg, Ww

NOTE:
Directions must be used as part of the Weekly Lesson Format. See page 6.

Lesson 2

TIP OF THE WEEK
Make certain your lowercase *e*'s and *i*'s are easily distinguishable. Poorly written, these two letters account for many spelling errors.

Day One Practice the following letters and words from this week's Scripture.

Dd

Despise

succeed

find

Day Two Continue practicing letters and words from this week's Scripture.

Gg

God's

spring

trouble

11

Copyright©2001 by Concerned Communications. All rights reserved.

✏ Extended Teaching

• To enhance understanding of this verse, ask students to define the word "despise" (to scorn, to regard with extreme dislike).

• Remind students that some lowercase letters have loops and some do not. Have them compare the loop letters *b, e, f, h, k,* and *l* with the non-loop letters *d, i,* and *t*. This exercise will be especially helpful for visual learners.

✏ For Discussion

"List some ways you can share God's Word with others." (using Scripture as you write letters, sharing Scripture Border Sheets, reading Scripture to elderly friends, etc.) "How can this help you succeed in life?" (make me sensitive to other's needs, teach me lasting principles, etc.)

Day Three *Continue practicing letters and words from this week's Scripture.*

Ww

Word

water

mountain

Day Four *Write this week's Scripture verse on a sheet of practice paper.*

Despise God's Word and find yourself in trouble. Obey it and succeed. The advice of a wise man reflects like water from a mountain spring.

Proverbs 13:13, 14

FOR DISCUSSION

List some ways you can share God's Word with others. How can this help you succeed in life?

12

Copyright©2001 by Concerned Communications. All rights reserved.

Scripture Verse

"How does a man become wise? The first step is to trust and reverence the Lord! Only fools refuse to be taught. Listen to your father and mother." Proverbs 1:7, 8

Tip of the Week

"For a car to drive smoothly, its wheels must be in proper alignment. Smooth handwriting requires proper alignment, too. Make sure your letters are on the line, not above or below it."

Letter Focus

Hh, Tt, Ll

NOTE:
Directions must be used as part of the Weekly Lesson Format. See page 6.

Lesson 3

TIP OF THE WEEK

For a car to drive smoothly, its wheels must be in proper alignment. Smooth handwriting requires proper alignment, too. Make sure your letters are on the line, not above or below it.

Day One Practice the following letters and words from this week's Scripture.

Hh

How

taught

mother

Day Two Continue practicing letters and words from this week's Scripture.

Tt

The

first

step

13

Copyright©2001 by Concerned Communications. All rights reserved.

Extended Teaching

• Using the board (or overhead projector), write an exaggerated example of letters above and below the line. This will quickly illustrate correct and incorrect alignment.

• Breaking the word *reverence* into parts offers excellent *e* connecting stroke practice: *re • ve • er • en • ce.*

• Draw attention to punctuation in this verse.

For Discussion

"How do we learn to trust someone?" (get to know them) "What does trusting God really mean?" (Answers will vary. For discussion: Point out that bungee-jumping takes a certain kind of trust. Even walking down the street takes a kind of trust! Ask students how trusting in God compares to these.)

Day Three Continue practicing letters and words from this week's Scripture.

L l

Lord

fools

Listen

Day Four Write this week's Scripture verse on a sheet of practice paper.

How does a man become wise?
The first step is to trust and
reverence the Lord! Only fools
refuse to be taught. Listen to your
father and mother.
                              Proverbs 1:7,8

FOR DISCUSSION
How do we learn to trust someone?
What does trusting God really mean?

14

Copyright©2001 by Concerned Communications. All rights reserved.

Lesson 4

Scripture Verse

"The Lord despises every kind of cheating. The character of even a child can be known by the way he acts—whether what he does is pure and right." Proverbs 20:10, 11

Tip of the Week

"Your name is the most important word you write. Write it with care on every paper you turn in. Even though your signature is unique, you should avoid unneccessary tails and frills."

Letter Focus

Cc, Ee, Rr

NOTE:
Directions must be used as part of the Weekly Lesson Format. See page 6.

Lesson 4

TIP OF THE WEEK

Your name is the most important word you write.
Write it with care on every paper you turn in. Even though
your signature is unique, you should avoid unneccessary tails and frills.

Day One Practice the following letters and words from this week's Scripture.

Cc

child

acts

character

Day Two Continue practicing letters and words from this week's Scripture.

Ee

even

cheating

whether

15

Copyright©2001 by Concerned Communications. All rights reserved.

✏ Extended Teaching

● For extra name practice, suggest students exchange autographs. Ask them to sign their name as if someone was looking for a person who'd inherited a great estate, and who could only be identified by their signature.

● Remind students that God's followers have a great inheritance — eternal life! (Fortunately God knows all of us by our hearts, not our handwriting!)

✏ For Discussion

"How do your actions reflect your character?" (kind hearts produce kind deeds) "Give at least two examples." (doing a task without being asked, being honest even when no one is looking, etc.)

Day Three Continue practicing letters and words from this week's Scripture.

Rr

right

every

pure

Day Four Write this week's Scripture verse on a sheet of practice paper.

The Lord despises every kind of cheating. The character of even a child can be known by the way he acts—whether what he does is pure and right.

Proverbs 20:10,11

FOR DISCUSSION
How do your actions reflect your character?
Give at least two examples.

16

Copyright©2001 by Concerned Communications. All rights reserved.

Lesson 5

Scripture Verse

"Just as a father punishes a son he delights in to make him better, so the Lord corrects you." Proverbs 3:12

Tip of the Week

"The capital letters *J*, *Y*, and *Z* fill the whole letter space. Make certain these letters touch the top line, and descend to the lower base line."

Letter Focus

Jj, Mm, Yy

NOTE:

Directions must be used as part of the Weekly Lesson Format. See page 6.

Lesson 5

TIP OF THE WEEK

The capital letters *J*, *Y*, and *Z* fill the whole letter space. Make certain these letters touch the top line, and descend to the lower base line.

Day One Practice the following letters and words from this week's Scripture.

Jj

Just

father

punishes

Day Two Continue practicing letters and words from this week's Scripture.

Mm

make

him

delights

17

Copyright©2001 by Concerned Communications. All rights reserved.

✏ Extended Teaching

● Show students how the tail letters *j* and *y* extend to the lower line. Then challenge students to identify the other tail letters: *f*, *g*, *p*, *q*, and *z*.

● Remind students that the capital letters *J*, *Y*, and *Z* are all connected to the rest of the word.

✏ For Discussion

"Are there bad ways to punish someone?" (critical, mean) "Are there good ways?" (firm, but caring) "Discuss the difference." (Read Hebrews 12:5-8 to the students. Remind them that rules can help teach self-control. Use a school rule as an illustration.)

Day Three Continue practicing letters and words from this week's Scripture.

Yy

you

corrects

son

Day Four Write this week's Scripture verse on a sheet of practice paper.

Just as a father punishes a son
he delights in to make him better,
so the Lord corrects you.
Proverbs 3:12

FOR DISCUSSION
Are there bad ways to punish someone? Are there good ways? Discuss the difference.

18

Copyright©2001 by Concerned Communications. All rights reserved.

Lesson 6

Scripture Verse

"It is an honor for a man to stay out of a fight. Only fools insist on quarreling." Proverbs 20:3

Tip of the Week

"The capitals *I* and *Q* are both upswing letters, just like the capital *J*. As you practice these letters this week, try to use the same slant for each one."

Letter Focus

Ii, Oo, Qq

NOTE:
Directions must be used as part of the Weekly Lesson Format. See page 6.

Lesson 6

TIP OF THE WEEK
The capitals *I* and *Q* are both upswing letters, just like the capital *J*. As you practice these letters this week, try to use the same slant for each one.

Day One   Practice the following letters and words from this week's Scripture.

Ii

It

insist

fight

Day Two   Continue practicing letters and words from this week's Scripture.

Oo

Only

honor

out

19

Copyright©2001 by Concerned Communications. All rights reserved.

Extended Teaching

- Students will benefit from practicing the *I* and *Q*. It will take some practice to write each smoothly.

- While the *O* and *Q* have similar shapes, they begin and end at different points on the line. These two letters show the importance of beginning letters at the correct point.

For Discussion

"Is fighting always a physical thing?" (some fights are with words) "List some good techniques for avoiding a fight." (walk away; try to see the other person's point of view; don't be overly sensitive)

Day Three Continue practicing letters and words from this week's Scripture.

Q q

quarreling

stay

man

Day Four Write this week's Scripture verse on a sheet of practice paper.

It is an honor for a man to stay out of a fight. Only fools insist on quarreling.

Proverbs 20:3

For Discussion
Is fighting always a physical thing?
List some good techniques for avoiding a fight.

20

Copyright©2001 by Concerned Communications. All rights reserved.

Lesson 7

Scripture Verse

"For the reverence and fear of God are basic to all wisdom. Knowing God results in every other kind of understanding." Proverbs 9:10

Tip of the Week

"This week, check the size of your letters. Using consistent size will make your letters look great, and your handwriting much easier to read."

Letter Focus

Ff, Bb, Kk

NOTE:
Directions must be used as part of the Weekly Lesson Format. See page 6.

Lesson 7

TIP OF THE WEEK
This week, check the size of your letters.
Using consistent size will make your letters
look great, and your handwriting much easier to read.

Day One Practice the following letters and words from this week's Scripture.

Ff
For

fear

wisdom

Day Two Continue practicing letters and words from this week's Scripture.

Bb
basic

reverence

results

21

Copyright©2001 by Concerned Communications. All rights reserved.

✏️ Extended Teaching

• Encourage students to keep letters a consistent, readable size. This age group has a tendency to begin using smaller letters.

• This would be a good verse for students to write in manuscript (either for practice or on a Scripture Border Sheet). Remind students that manuscript handwriting is a life skill, and must be maintained.

✏️ For Discussion

"What does the word 'fear' mean in this verse?" (respect, awe) "How does knowing God result in deeper understanding?" (God is the source of knowledge. As we understand God better, our understanding of life expands.)

Day Three Continue practicing letters and words from this week's Scripture.

Kk

Knowing

kind

understanding

Day Four Write this week's Scripture verse on a sheet of practice paper.

For the reverence and fear of God are basic to all wisdom. Knowing God results in every other kind of understanding.

Proverbs 9:10

FOR DISCUSSION
What does the word "fear" mean in this verse? How does knowing God result in deeper understanding?

22

Copyright©2001 by Concerned Communications. All rights reserved.

Lesson 8

Scripture Verse

"Telling lies about someone is as harmful as hitting him with an axe, or wounding him with a sword, or shooting him with a sharp arrow."
Proverbs 25:18

Tip of the Week

"This week's focus letters are the 'boatstroke' capitals *T* and *S*. Boatstroke capitals are not joined to the rest of the word. Can you identify other boatstroke capitals?" (*B, F, G, I*)

Letter Focus

Tt, Xx, Ss

NOTE:
Directions must be used as part of the Weekly Lesson Format. See page 6.

Lesson 8

TIP OF THE WEEK
This week's focus letters are the "boatstoke" capitals
T and *S*. Boatstroke capitals are not joined to the rest of the word.
Can you identify the other boatstoke capitals? (Hint: There are four more.)

Day One — Practice the following letters and words from this week's Scripture.

Tt

Telling

hitting

with

Day Two — Continue practicing letters and words from this week's Scripture.

Xx

axe

harmful

wounding

23

Copyright©2001 by Concerned Communications. All rights reserved.

✏ Extended Teaching

• Remind students that the capital $\mathcal{X}$ is one of four two-stroke capital letters. The others are $\mathcal{H}$, $\mathcal{K}$, and $\mathcal{T}$.

• The lowercase x is also a two-stroke letter. The words *except*, *excellent*, and *exit* are great x practice words because each word contains at least one other letter requiring a second stroke after the word is written.

✏ For Discussion

"How are lies and criticism of others harmful?" (lies can ruin reputations, etc.—see Ephesians 4:25) "What is the opposite approach?" (praise and encouragement—see Ephesians 4:29)

Day Three Continue practicing letters and words from this week's Scripture.

Ss

sword

shooting

sharp

Day Four Write this week's Scripture verse on a sheet of practice paper.

Telling lies about someone is as harmful as hitting him with an axe, or wounding him with a sword, or shooting him with a sharp arrow.

Proverbs 25:18

FOR DISCUSSION

How are lies and criticism of others harmful?
What is the opposite approach?

24

Copyright©2001 by Concerned Communications. All rights reserved.

Scripture Verse

"It is better to get your hands dirty—and eat, than to be too proud to work and starve. Hard work means prosperity. Only a fool idles away his time." Proverbs 12:9, 11

Tip of the Week

Lesson Tip: "Bridges connect one bank of the river to the other. 'Bridgestrokes' help us connect one part of a word to another. This week's bridgestroke letters are *b, o, v,* and *w.*"

Letter Focus

A a, P p, V v

NOTE:
Directions must be used as part of the Weekly Lesson Format. See page 6.

Lesson 9

TIP OF THE WEEK
Bridges connect one bank of the river to the other. "Bridgestrokes" help us connect one part of a word to another. This week's bridgestroke letters are *b, o, v,* and *w.*

Day One Practice the following letters and words from this week's Scripture.

A a

away

hands

idles

Day Two Continue practicing letters and words from this week's Scripture.

P p

prosperity

better

dirty

25

Copyright©2001 by Concerned Communications. All rights reserved.

Extended Teaching

● Extra practice of the bridgestroke letter combinations from this verse (*be, ou, oo, or, wa, wo, re*) would be beneficial.

● Challenge your students to be creative in coloring their Scripture Border Sheets. A classroom contest for the most creative or unusual border sheet often brings surprising results.

For Discussion

"What are some ways people foolishly idle away their time?" (watching TV, playing video games, etc.) "Name some situations where hard work can really pay off." (improved grades, cleaner environment, etc.)

Day Three Continue practicing letters and words from this week's Scripture.

Vr

starve

proud

work

Day Four Write this week's Scripture verse on a sheet of practice paper.

It is better to get your hands dirty—and eat, than to be too proud to work and starve. Hard work means prosperity. Only a fool idles away his time.

Proverbs 12:9, 11

FOR DISCUSSION
What are some ways people foolishly idle away their time? Name some situations where hard work can really pay off.

26

Copyright©2001 by Concerned Communications. All rights reserved.

Lesson 10

Scripture Verse

"Take a lesson from the ants, you lazy fellow. Learn from their ways and be wise! They labor hard all summer, gathering food for the winter." Proverbs 6:6, 8

Tip of the Week

"As you practice the capital and lowercase *Z* this week, watch for their similarities and differences. Can you identify other similar letter pairs?" (*A a, C c, O o, U u, V v, W w, X x,* and *Y y*)

Letter Focus

Zz, Tt, Ll

NOTE:
Directions must be used as part of the Weekly Lesson Format. See page 6.

Lesson 10

TIP OF THE WEEK

As you practice the capital and lowercase *Z* this week, watch for their similarities and differences. Can you identify other similar letter pairs? (Hint: there are at least six more.)

Day One Practice the following letters and words from this week's Scripture.

Zz

lazy

ways

winter

Day Two Continue practicing letters and words from this week's Scripture.

Tt

Take

gathering

ants

27

Copyright©2001 by Concerned Communications. All rights reserved.

✏️ Extended Teaching

● The lower case *y* is an overstroke letter in a group that includes *m, n, v, y, x,* and *z*. Talking about and emphasizing similarities such as these can be very helpful to both auditory and visual learners.

● One book in the Old Testament was written by the prophet Zechariah. Challenge your students to use a Bible Dictionary to discover other names beginning with *Z*.

✏️ For Discussion

"What did Solomon mean when he told us to learn from the ants?" (hard work usually pays off) "What are some other lessons we can learn from nature?" (Answers will vary. Example: Bees all have special talents—worker, scout, nurse. So do people!)

Day Three Continue practicing letters and words from this week's Scripture.

L l

Learn

fellow

lesson

Day Four Write this week's Scripture verse on a sheet of practice paper.

Take a lesson from the ants, you lazy fellow. Learn from their ways and be wise! They labor hard all summer, gathering food for the winter.

Proverbs 6:6, 8

FOR DISCUSSION
What did Solomon mean when he told us to learn from the ants? What are some other lessons we can learn from nature?

28

Copyright©2001 by Concerned Communications. All rights reserved.

Lesson 11

✏ Scripture Verse

"From a wise mind comes careful and persuasive speech. Kind words are like honey—enjoyable and healthful." Proverbs 16:23, 24

✏ Tip of the Week

"Posture and paper position make a difference. Make sure your feet are flat on the floor, and your back is straight. Lean slightly forward, with your paper slanted in the direction of your writing arm."

✏ Letter Focus

Ff, Pp, Kk

NOTE:
Directions must be used as part of the Weekly Lesson Format. See page 6.

Lesson 11

TIP OF THE WEEK
Posture and paper position make a big difference.
Make sure your feet are flat on the floor, and your back is straight.
Lean slightly forward, with your paper slanted in the direction of your writing arm.

Day One Practice the following letters and words from this week's Scripture.

Ff
From

healthful

careful

Day Two Continue practicing letters and words from this week's Scripture.

Pp
persuasive

speech

comes

29

Copyright©2001 by Concerned Communications. All rights reserved.

✏ Extended Teaching

● Point out that *f* and *k* are loop letters. Other loop letters include *b*, *e*, *h*, and *l*.

● Encourage students to practice correct number formation. Numbers are written with one stroke—with the exception of the number *4*.

✏ For Discussion

"List some ways we can make our words 'like honey.'" (appreciation words, praise words, polite words.) Make an extra effort to talk softly and kindly this week." (For discussion: Ask students "What is the difference between appropriate 'honey-coated' words and 'smooth talking'?" Clue: Motivation.)

Day Three   Continue practicing letters and words from this week's Scripture.

K k

Kind

like

enjoyable

Day Four   Write this week's Scripture verse on a sheet of practice paper.

From a wise mind comes careful and persuasive speech. Kind words are like honey—enjoyable and healthful.

Proverbs 16:23, 24

FOR DISCUSSION
List some ways we can make our words "like honey." Make an extra effort to talk softly and kindly this week.

30

Copyright©2001 by Concerned Communications. All rights reserved.

Lesson 12

Scripture Verse

"Your own soul is nourished when you are kind; it is destroyed when you are cruel. . .the good man's reward lasts forever." Proverbs 11:17, 18

Tip of the Week

"Here's a way to check your letter slant: Draw a line through the downstrokes. If your slant is consistent, the lines will be parallel. How does *your* slant measure up?" (Although writing slant may vary slightly from student to student, each student's individual slant needs to be consistent.)

Letter Focus

Yy, Nn, Rr

NOTE:
Directions must be used as part of the Weekly Lesson Format. See page 6.

Lesson 12

TIP OF THE WEEK
Here's a way to check your slant: Draw a line through the downstrokes. If your slant is consistent, the lines will be parallel. How does *your* slant measure up?

Day One Practice the following letters and words from this week's Scripture.

Yy
Your

destroyed

soul

Day Two Continue practicing letters and words from this week's Scripture.

Nn
nourished

own

cruel

31

Copyright©2001 by Concerned Communications. All rights reserved.

✏ Extended Teaching

• In addition to the $\mathcal{Y}$ and $\mathcal{N}$, extra practice of the other cane stroke capitals ($\mathcal{H}, \mathcal{K}, \mathcal{M}, \mathcal{U}, \mathcal{V}, \mathcal{W}$, and $\mathcal{X}$) can be beneficial.

• Choose two teams and ask them to write down proper names or towns or people that begin with these cane stroke capitals. The Bible Dictionary is a good source for names of places and people.

✏ For Discussion

"Discuss the concept of 'random acts of kindness.' Watch for such opportunities at school this week. Remember, your kind act is a secret! Don't let anyone know!"

Day Three   Continue practicing letters and words from this week's Scripture.

Rr

reward

are

forever

Day Four   Write this week's Scripture verse on a sheet of practice paper.

Your own soul is nourished when you are kind; it is destroyed when you are cruel...the good man's reward lasts forever.

Proverbs 11:17,18

FOR DISCUSSION
Discuss the concept of "random acts of kindness."
Watch for such opportunities at school this week.
Remember, your kind act is a secret!
Don't let anyone know!

32

Copyright©2001 by Concerned Communications. All rights reserved.

Lesson 13

✏ Scripture Verse

"A soft answer turns away wrath, but harsh words cause quarrels. Gentle words cause life and health: griping brings discouragement."
Proverbs 15:1, 4

✏ Tip of the Week

"This week's verse contains all the lowercase oval letters (a, c, d, g, o, p and q). Make certain they are well rounded, and that the oval portion fills the letter space."

✏ Letter Focus

Cc, Gg, Qq

NOTE:
Directions must be used as part of the Weekly Lesson Format. See page 6.

Lesson 13

✏ TIP OF THE WEEK
This week's verse contains all the lowercase oval letters (a, c, d, g, o, p and q). Make certain they are well rounded, and that the oval portion fills the letter space.

Day One Practice the following letters and words from this week's Scripture.

Cc

cause

discouragement

answer

Day Two Continue practicing letters and words from this week's Scripture.

Gg

Gentle

griping

brings

33

Copyright©2001 by Concerned Communications. All rights reserved.

✏ Extended Teaching

• Point out that the oval capital groups includes the letter C as well as a, E, and O.

• While p is an oval letter, it does not begin with an oval stroke. The p and q both have tails, but they are written with a different beginning and ending stroke. By contrast, the c is left open.

✏ For Discussion

"Think of a situation where there were critical or harsh words. Now imagine that same scene with positive, kind words. Describe the difference between the two." (Answers will vary. You may wish to do a role play to demonstrate. Example: a student responds to a player whose mistake cost the team points.)

Day Three Continue practicing letters and words from this week's Scripture.

Q q

quarrels

harsh

soft

Day Four Write this week's Scripture verse on a sheet of practice paper.

A soft answer turns away wrath, but harsh words cause quarrels. Gentle words cause life and health; griping brings discouragement.

Proverbs 15:1,4

FOR DISCUSSION
Think of a situation where there were critical or harsh words. Now imagine that same scene with positive, kind words. Describe the difference between the two.

34

Copyright©2001 by Concerned Communications. All rights reserved.

Lesson 14

Scripture Verse

"Everyone enjoys giving good advice, and how wonderful it is to be able to say the right thing at the right time! The road of the godly leads upward." Proverbs 15:23, 24

Tip of the Week

"How you hold your pencil when you write is very important! If your wrist gets tired, you may be holding your pencil too tightly. Move your wrist in a circular motion to relax your hand."

Letter Focus

Ee, Jj, Oo

NOTE:
Directions must be used as part of the Weekly Lesson Format. See page 6.

TIP OF THE WEEK
How you hold your pencil when you write is very important! If your wrist gets tired, you may be holding your pencil too tightly. Move your wrist in a circular motion to relax your hand.

Day One Practice the following letters and words from this week's Scripture.

Ee

Everyone

time

advice

Day Two Continue practicing letters and words from this week's Scripture.

Jj

enjoys

upward

giving

35

Copyright©2001 by Concerned Communications. All rights reserved.

Extended Teaching

• When students grip their pencils too tightly, it not only tires their wrists, but often results in very heavy writing. Watch for students who stop and shake their hand after writing. Encourage a more relaxed grip.

• Practice wrist-relaxing exercises. Have students shake their hands from the wrist in a rag doll manner, or have them rotate their wrists in a circular motion.

For Discussion

"Can you think of a story or situation where someone said 'the right thing at the right time'? Describe it." (Answers will vary. Remind students that when a classmate gives a wrong answer and others are tempted to laugh, an encouraging word can help ease the situation.)

Day Three Continue practicing letters and words from this week's Scripture.

Oo

wonderful

road

godly

Day Four Write this week's Scripture verse on a sheet of practice paper.

Everyone enjoys giving good advice, and how wonderful it is to be able to say the right thing at the right time! The road of the godly leads upward.

Proverbs 15:23, 24

For Discussion

Can you think of a story or situation where someone said "the right thing at the right time"? Describe it.

36

Copyright©2001 by Concerned Communications. All rights reserved.

Lesson 15

✏ Scripture Verse

"It is better to be slow-tempered than famous; it is better to have self-control than to control an army." Proverbs 16:32

✏ Tip of the Week

"Putting a hyphen between two words can modify their meaning. Look at this week's hyphenated words. What is the meaning of each separate word? How does the hyphen change the meaning?" (slow-tempered, self-control, etc.)

✏ Letter Focus

Ss, Uu, Vv

NOTE:
Directions must be used as part of the Weekly Lesson Format. See page 6.

Lesson 15

TIP OF THE WEEK
Putting a hyphen between two words can modify their meaning. Look at this week's hyphenated words. What is the meaning of each separate word? How does the hyphen change the meaning?

Day One Practice the following letters and words from this week's Scripture.

Ss

slow

is

self-control

Day Two Continue practicing letters and words from this week's Scripture.

Uu

famous

army

than

37

Copyright©2001 by Concerned Communications. All rights reserved.

Extended Teaching

• Point out the similarities and differences between the lowercase *v*, *u*, and *w*. Remind students that upstroke letters *u* and *w* can easily be misread if not written correctly. Ask students to identify and write the other upstroke letters (*i*, *j*, *p*, *r*, *s*, *t*).

• Point out that the capitals *S* and *G* begin with the same upswing stroke.

For Discussion

"List some situations that might give an opportunity to demonstrate self-control." (possible answers could relate to anger, temptation, personal issues, etc.) "How can we learn to become slow-tempered?" (think of a good general response ahead of time, ask God to help you control your temper, etc.)

Day Three Continue practicing letters and words from this week's Scripture.

Vv

have

slow-tempered

control

Day Four Write this week's Scripture verse on a sheet of practice paper.

It is better to be slow-tempered than famous; it is better to have self-control than to control an army.

Proverbs 16:32

For Discussion
List some situations that might give an opportunity to demonstrate self-control. How can we learn to become "slow-tempered"?

38

Copyright©2001 by Concerned Communications. All rights reserved.

Lesson 16

Scripture Verse

"A happy face means a glad heart; a sad face means a breaking heart. When a man is gloomy, everything seems to go wrong; when he is cheerful everything seems right!" Proverbs 15:13, 15

Tip of the Week

"Punctuation often changes the meaning of a sentence. This week's verse contains many types of punctuation. Can you name and correctly use each type?" (semi-colon, period, comma, exclamation point, colon)

Letter Focus

Ww, Cc, Yy

NOTE:
Directions must be used as part of the Weekly Lesson Format. See page 6.

Lesson 16

TIP OF THE WEEK

Punctuation often changes the meaning of a sentence. This week's verse contains many types of punctuation. Can you name and correctly use each type? (Hint: Five types of punctuation are used.)

Day One Practice the following letters and words from this week's Scripture.

Ww
When
wrong
breaking

Day Two Continue practicing letters and words from this week's Scripture.

Cc
face
seems
means

39

Copyright©2001 by Concerned Communications. All rights reserved.

✏ Extended Teaching

● Use the following example to expand on the Lesson Tip: "Today is Tuesday. This simple sentence changes greatly with punctuation. Replace the period with a question mark, and it appears that you're not sure what day it is! Replace it with an explanation mark, and then it becomes a special day you've been waiting for—perhaps a birthday! What a difference!"

✏ For Discussion

"What does the phrase 'look on the bright side' mean? How can our outlook affect our attitude?" (we tend to find what we're looking for, if we're negative it can make others respond negatively, etc.)

Day Three Continue practicing letters and words from this week's Scripture.

Yy

everything

gloomy

glad

Day Four Write this week's Scripture verse on a sheet of practice paper.

A happy face means a glad heart; a sad face means a breaking heart. When a man is gloomy, everything seems to go wrong; when he is cheerful everything seems right!

Proverbs 15:13, 15

FOR DISCUSSION
What does the phrase "look on the bright side" mean? How can our outlook affect our attitude?

40

Copyright©2001 by Concerned Communications. All rights reserved.

Lesson 17

✏ Scripture Verse

"Timely advice is as lovely as golden apples in a silver basket. Be patient and you will finally win, for a soft tongue can break hard bones."
Proverbs 25:11, 15

✏ Tip of the Week

"The capital $\mathcal{B}$, $\mathcal{P}$, and $\mathcal{R}$ all have the same foward oval stroke. Focus on making this common stroke the same as you write each letter."

✏ Letter Focus

$\mathcal{B}b$, $\mathcal{P}p$, $\mathcal{R}r$

NOTE:
Directions must be used as part of the Weekly Lesson Format. See page 6.

Lesson 17

Tip of the week
The capital $\mathcal{B}$, $\mathcal{P}$, and $\mathcal{R}$ all have the same forward oval stroke. Focus on making this common stroke the same as you write each letter.

Day One — Practice the following letters and words from this week's Scripture.

$\mathcal{B}b$

$\mathcal{B}e$

bones

basket

Day Two — Continue practicing letters and words from this week's Scripture.

$\mathcal{P}p$

patient

apples

tongue

41

Copyright©2001 by Concerned Communications. All rights reserved.

✏ Extended Teaching

● Remind students that boatstroke capitals do not connect to the rest of the word—like the capital $\mathcal{B}$ in this lesson.

● Point out that the letter $\mathcal{P}$ is used in every lesson this year since the Scripture verses are all from the book of Proverbs.

✏ For Discussion

"What are some ways that patience can benefit us? How can we learn to be patient?" (Answers will vary. For discussion: Someone once said, "Sometimes when you win, you lose!" Ask the students what they think this might mean. Example: winning an argument, but losing a friend.)

Day Three Continue practicing letters and words from this week's Scripture.

Rr

break

hard

Timely

Day Four Write this week's Scripture verse on a sheet of practice paper.

Timely advice is as lovely as golden apples in a silver basket. Be patient and you will finally win, for a soft tongue can break hard bones.

Proverbs 25:11,15

FOR DISCUSSION
What are some ways that patience can benefit us? How can we learn to be more patient?

42

Copyright©2001 by Concerned Communications. All rights reserved.

Scripture Verse

"Don't talk so much. You keep putting your foot in your mouth. Be sensible and turn off the flow. . .The words of fools are a dime a dozen." Proverbs 10: 19, 20

Tip of the Week

"All the lowercase tall letters are contained in this verse. Make certain that these letters all touch the top line. Also, notice that two of these letters are written without loops." (*d* and *t*)

Letter Focus

Dd, Ff, Zz

NOTE:
Directions must be used as part of the Weekly Lesson Format. See page 6.

TIP OF THE WEEK

All the lowercase tall letters are contained in this verse. Make certain that these letters all touch the top line. Also, notice that two of these letters are written without loops.

Lesson 18

Day One Practice the following letters and words from this week's Scripture.

Dd

Don't

and

dime

Day Two Continue practicing letters and words from this week's Scripture.

Ff

flow

foot

fools

43

Copyright©2001 by Concerned Communications. All rights reserved.

Extended Teaching

● In addition to this week's verse, students may benefit from reading other texts about the tongue. See Proverbs 12:18 and James 3:4, 5.

● Have students critique their own writing, looking specifically at letter size and how letters fill the space.

For Discussion

"Do others think you talk too much, or not enough? What do your parents and friends think? What are some ways we can regulate our speech?" (Answers will vary—See Ecclesiastes 3:1, 7.)

Day Three Continue practicing letters and words from this week's Scripture.

Zz

dozen

sensible

putting

Day Four Write this week's Scripture verse on a sheet of practice paper.

Don't talk so much. You keep putting your foot in your mouth. Be sensible and turn off the flow... The words of fools are a dime a dozen.

Proverbs 10:19, 20

FOR DISCUSSION

Do others think you talk too much, or not enough? What do your parents and friends think? What are some ways we can regulate our speech?

44

Copyright©2001 by Concerned Communications. All rights reserved.

Scripture Verse

"Telling the truth gives a man great satisfaction, and hard work returns many blessings to him. Truth stands the test of time; lies are soon exposed." Proverbs 12:14, 19

Tip of the Week

"For more efficient writing, remember to dot the *i*'s and cross the *t*'s and *x*'s *after* you've written the entire word. This will make your writing smoother."

Letter Focus

Tt, Xx, Aa

NOTE:
Directions must be used as part of the Weekly Lesson Format. See page 6.

TIP OF THE WEEK
For more efficient writing, remember to dot the *i*'s and cross the *t*'s and *x*'s *after* you've written the entire word. This will make your writing smoother.

Lesson 19

Day One Practice the following letters and words from this week's Scripture.

Tt

Telling

Truth

test

Day Two Continue practicing letters and words from this week's Scripture.

Xx

exposed

gives

blessings

45

Copyright©2001 by Concerned Communications. All rights reserved.

Extended Teaching

• The focus letter $\mathcal{A}$ is an oval capital. Other letters to practice in this letter group are $\mathcal{C}$, $\mathcal{E}$, and $\mathcal{O}$. Ask students how these capitals are alike and different.

• A great way to practice connecting strokes is by having students write any lowercase letter in groups of three. (*aaa*, *xxx*, etc.)

For Discussion

"Can you 'tell the truth' even without speaking? What do your actions say? Give examples." (Kind, gentle actions tell others "the truth" about God's character, etc.)

Day Three   Continue practicing letters and words from this week's Scripture.

A a

great

many

satisfaction

Day Four   Write this week's Scripture verse on a sheet of practice paper.

Telling the truth gives a man great satisfaction, and hard work returns many blessings to him. Truth stands the test of time; lies are soon exposed.

Proverbs 12:14, 19

FOR DISCUSSION
Can you "tell the truth" even without speaking? What do your actions say? Give examples.

46

Copyright©2001 by Concerned Communications. All rights reserved.

Lesson 20

Scripture Verse

"If you want a long and satisfying life, closely follow My instructions. Never forget to be truthful and kind. Hold these virtues tightly. Write them deep within your heart." Proverbs 3:2, 3

Tip of the Week

"Critique a classmate's paper this week, using the **Five Star** evaluation (letter alignment, shape, size, slant, and spacing). Be sure your critique is kind and constructive."

Letter Focus

Nn, Hh, Kk

NOTE:
Directions must be used as part of the Weekly Lesson Format. See page 6.

Lesson 20

TIP OF THE WEEK
Critique a classmate's paper this week, using the **Five Star** evaluation (letter alignment, shape, size, slant, and spacing). Be sure your critique is kind and constructive.

Day One Practice the following letters and words from this week's Scripture.

Nn
Never
within
instructions

Day Two Continue practicing letters and words from this week's Scripture.

Hh
Hold
truthful
heart

47

Copyright©2001 by Concerned Communications. All rights reserved.

Extended Teaching

- All this week's focus capitals are cane stroke letters. Remind students that the cane needs to be leaning slightly!

- In this week's verse, the capital letters M and N connect to the rest of the word; the I, P, and W do not.

- Point out that the lowercase h and k can be easily confused if not written correctly.

For Discussion

"List some ways you can show kindness to your friends. . .your family. . .your neighbors. How does being kind make you feel inside?" (Answers will vary.)

Day Three   Continue practicing letters and words from this week's Scripture.

K k

kind

satisfying

tightly

Day Four   Write this week's Scripture verse on a sheet of practice paper.

If you want a long and satisfying life, closely follow My instructions. Never forget to be truthful and kind. Hold these virtues tightly. Write them deep within your heart.

Proverbs 3:2,3

FOR DISCUSSION

List some ways you can show kindness to your friends. . . your family. . .your neighbors. How does being kind make you feel inside?

48

Copyright©2001 by Concerned Communications. All rights reserved.

Lesson 21

Scripture Verse

Scripture Verse

"It is hard to stop a quarrel once it starts, so don't let it begin. The Lord despises those who say that bad is good, and good is bad."
Proverbs 17:14, 15

Tip of the Week

"What two letters almost always go together?" (*q* and *u*) "As you practice the *qu* combination this week, think of other words that use this combination."

Letter Focus

Ii, Qq, Oo

NOTE:
Directions must be used as part of the Weekly Lesson Format. See page 6.

Lesson 21

TIP OF THE WEEK

What two letters almost always go together?
(Hint: you have to be "quick" to get this!) As you practice the
qu combination this week, think of other words that use this combination.

Day One Practice the following letters and words from this week's Scripture.

Ii

It

despises

begin

Day Two Continue practicing letters and words from this week's Scripture.

Qq
quarrel

starts

bad

49

Copyright©2001 by Concerned Communications. All rights reserved.

✏️ Extended Teaching

● Since the capital Q is not often used, students may benefit from extra practice of words like: *Quincy, Quebec, Queens*.

● Point out that the same upswing beginning stroke is part of the *I* and *Q*. This verse also contains the lowercase oval letters: *a, c, d, g, o,* and *q*. The shape of these letters determines their readability.

✏️ For Discussion

"What are some ways to stop a quarrel from beginning?" (see also Lesson 6) "In what way can our character help prevent quarrels?" (harder to quarrel with someone who demonstrates gentleness, goodness, patience, etc.)

Day Three Continue practicing letters and words from this week's Scripture.

Oo

once

stop

those

Day Four Write this week's Scripture verse on a sheet of practice paper.

It is hard to stop a quarrel once it starts, so don't let it begin. The Lord despises those who say that bad is good, and good is bad.

Proverbs 17:14, 15

For Discussion

What are some ways to stop a quarrel from beginning? In what way can our character help prevent quarrels?

50

Copyright©2001 by Concerned Communications. All rights reserved.

Lesson 22

✏ Scripture Verse

"A cheerful heart does good like medicine, but a broken spirit makes one sick." Proverbs 17:22

✏ Tip of the Week

"Focus on letter spacing and letter size this week. Consistency in these two skills helps give your handwriting a balanced look, and makes it easier to read."

✏ Letter Focus

Ss, Mm, Uu

NOTE:
Directions must be used as part of the Weekly Lesson Format. See page 6.

Lesson 22

TIP OF THE WEEK

Focus on letter spacing and letter size this week. Consistency in these two skills helps give your handwriting a balanced look, and makes it easier to read.

Day One — Practice the following letters and words from this week's Scripture.

Ss

spirit

sick

does

Day Two — Continue practicing letters and words from this week's Scripture.

Mm

medicine

makes

good

51

Copyright©2001 by Concerned Communications. All rights reserved.

✏ Extended Teaching

● Encourage students to practice this week's verse in manuscript (printing). Challenge them to print like a computer—consistent letters, spacing, and size.

● Students may practice the letter combinations *er*, *ar*, *ir*, and *or*. These combinations are challenging due to the loop/non-loop contrast, as well as the points on the letter *r*.

✏ For Discussion

"What are some outward signs of a cheerful heart? A broken spirit? How should we respond when we see these signs in others?" (If you think a friend is depressed or in trouble, don't be afraid to ask for help, etc.)

Day Three Continue practicing letters and words from this week's Scripture.

Uu

but

cheerful

broken

Day Four Write this week's Scripture verse on a sheet of practice paper.

A cheerful heart does good like medicine, but a broken spirit makes one sick.

Proverbs 17:22

FOR DISCUSSION
What are some outward signs of a cheerful heart?
What might show a broken spirit? How should
we respond when we see these signs in others?

52

Copyright©2001 by Concerned Communications. All rights reserved.

Scripture Verse

"If you want favor with both God and man, and a reputation for good judgment and common sense, then trust the Lord completely; don't ever trust yourself." Proverbs 3:4, 5

Tip of the Week

"The capital letters $\mathcal{E}$, $\mathcal{Z}$, and C are our focus this week. Think of the name of a person or place that begins with each of these letters." (Esther, Ethiopia, Zarephath, Zeri, Christ, Cyprus, etc.) "Just for fun, practice writing these names, as well as others."

Letter Focus

Ee, Zz, Cc

NOTE:
Directions must be used as part of the Weekly Lesson Format. See page 6.

Lesson 23

TIP OF THE WEEK
The capital letters $\mathcal{E}$, $\mathcal{Z}$, and C are our focus this week.
Think of the name of a person or place that begins with each of these letters. Just for fun, practice writing these names as well as others.

Day One Practice the following letters and words from this week's Scripture.

Ee

sense

ever

reputation

Day Two Continue practicing letters and words from this week's Scripture.

Zz
Zion

want

judgment

53

Copyright©2001 by Concerned Communications. All rights reserved.

✏️ Extended Teaching

• Remind students that the *z* is an overstroke letter. Other letters to practice from this group are: *m*, *n*, *v*, *x*, and *y*.

• Your students may enjoy consulting a Bible dictionary to find the names of people and places beginning with the letters *E*, *I*, and *C*. Note that these three capitals are connected to the rest of the word.

✏️ For Discussion

"In order to really trust someone, you have to know them very well. What are some of the ways we can get to know God better?" (read about God, spend time in prayer, spend time in nature, fellowship with others who know God, etc.)

Day Three Continue practicing letters and words from this week's Scripture.

Cc

completely

common

trust

Day Four Write this week's Scripture verse on a sheet of practice paper.

If you want favor with both
God and man, and a reputation
for good judgment and common
sense, then trust the Lord
completely; don't ever trust
yourself.
Proverbs 3:4,5

FOR DISCUSSION
In order to really trust someone, you have to know them very well. What are some of the ways we can get to know God better?

54

Copyright©2001 by Concerned Communications. All rights reserved.

Lesson 24

✏ Scripture Verse

"If you must choose, take a good name rather than great riches; for to be held in loving esteem is better than silver and gold."
Proverbs 22:1

✏ Tip of the Week

"This verse contains all the lowercase loop letters. As you write the words, make certain you only place loops where they belong. Also, review your posture and paper position this week."

✏ Letter Focus

Ll, Rr, Hh

NOTE:
Directions must be used as part of the Weekly Lesson Format. See page 6.

Lesson 24

✏ **TIP OF THE WEEK**
This verse contains all the lowercase loop letters.
As you write the words, make certain you only place loops
where they belong. Also, review your posture and paper position this week.

Day One **Practice the following letters and words from this week's Scripture.**

L l

loving

gold

esteem

Day Two **Continue practicing letters and words from this week's Scripture.**

Rr

rather

riches

silver

55

Copyright©2001 by Concerned Communications. All rights reserved.

✏ Extended Teaching

● Remind students that their writing paper should be slanted the same direction as their writing arm (see page 9).

● Encourage students to rewrite the verse of the week in their own words. (Example: "If I had to choose between being rich or having a good reputation, I'd have to admit that a good name is more important.")

✏ For Discussion

"How do our actions affect what others think of us? Does our relationship with God impact our behavior? In what way?" (Answers will vary. For discussion: "What does this phrase mean—Your actions speak louder than your words?")

Day Three Continue practicing letters and words from this week's Scripture.

Hh

held

choose

must

Day Four Write this week's Scripture verse on a sheet of practice paper.

If you must choose, take a good name rather than great riches; for to be held in loving esteem is better than silver and gold.

Proverbs 22:1

FOR DISCUSSION

How do our actions affect what others think of us? Does our relationship with God impact our behavior? In what way?

56

Copyright©2001 by Concerned Communications. All rights reserved.

Lesson 25

Scripture Verse

"A mirror reflects a man's face, but what he is really like is shown by the kind of friends he chooses." Proverbs 27:19

Tip of the Week

"To drive a car properly, you have to keep it between the lines! Handwriting alignment is a lot like that. Take extra care this week to keep your letters and words between the lines."

Letter Focus

Bb, Ss, Yy

NOTE:

Directions must be used as part of the Weekly Lesson Format. See page 6.

Lesson 25

TIP OF THE WEEK

To drive a car properly, you have to keep it
between the lines! Handwriting alignment is a lot like that.
Take extra care this week to keep your letters and words between the lines!

Day One Practice the following letters and words from this week's Scripture.

Bb

but

by

mirror

Day Two Continue practicing letters and words from this week's Scripture.

Ss

shown

friends

reflects

57

Copyright©2001 by Concerned Communications. All rights reserved.

✏ Extended Teaching

● This verse contains several bridgestroke letter combinations. Students will find it beneficial to practice these. They are *bu, or, os, ov, ve, wh,* and *un*.

● Remind students that the letters *r* and *s* are written with distinctive points.

✏ For Discussion

"Think about your closest friends. What are they really like? How is this similar or different from what you'd like to become?" (Answers will vary.)

Day Three   Continue practicing letters and words from this week's Scripture.

Yy

really

what

chooses

Day Four   Write this week's Scripture verse on a sheet of practice paper.

A mirror reflects a man's face, but what he is really like is shown by the kind of friends he chooses.

Proverbs 27:19

FOR DISCUSSION
Think about your closest friends. What are they really like? How is this similar or different from what you'd like to become?

58

Copyright©2001 by Concerned Communications. All rights reserved.

Lesson 26

✏ Scripture Verse

"Wisdom is a tree of life to those who eat her fruit; happy is the man who keeps on eating it." Proverbs 3:18

✏ Tip of the Week

"Few verses contain *x* words, yet the *x* is still an important letter to practice! Proverbs 4:8, 9 is similar to this week's verse, so we borrowed an *x* word from it for our practice this week."

✏ Letter Focus

Pp, Dd, Xx

NOTE:
Directions must be used as part of the Weekly Lesson Format. See page 6.

Lesson 26

Tip of the week
Few verses contain *x* words, yet the *x* is still
an important letter to practice! Proverbs 4: 8, 9 is similar to this
week's verse, so we borrowed an *x* word from it for our practice this week.

Day One Practice the following letters and words from this week's Scripture.

Pp

Proverbs

happy

keeps

Day Two Continue practicing letters and words from this week's Scripture.

Dd

Wisdom

who

eating

59

Copyright©2001 by Concerned Communications. All rights reserved.

✏️ Extended Teaching

● Ask your students to compare Proverbs 4: 8, 9 with this week's verse. It says "If you exalt wisdom, she will exalt you. Hold her fast and she will lead you to great honor."

● Remind students that the tail letters *p* and *f* both contain loops that extend to the lower line.

✏️ For Discussion

"List some ways we can 'eat' wisdom." (following good advice; applying what we read; looking for ways to improve; etc.) "What is the difference between wisdom and knowledge?" (knowledge means knowing or being aware of something; collecting facts. . .wisdom implies using those facts wisely; using good judgment.)

Day Three   Continue practicing letters and words from this week's Scripture.

Xx

exalt

tree

fruit

Day Four   Write this week's Scripture verse on a sheet of practice paper.

Wisdom is a tree of life to those who eat her fruit; happy is the man who keeps on eating it.
                                Proverbs 3:18

🔊 **FOR DISCUSSION**
List some ways we can "eat" wisdom.
What is the difference between
wisdom and knowledge?

60

Copyright©2001 by Concerned Communications. All rights reserved.

Lesson 27

Scripture Verse

"Don't be conceited, sure of your own wisdom. Instead, trust and reverence the Lord, and turn your back on evil; when you do that, then you will be given renewed health and vitality." Proverbs 3:7, 8

Tip of the Week

"The 'overstroke' is easy to identify in letters like *n* and *m*. Watch for other overstroke letters as you practice this week." (The *n*, *m*, *v*, and *y* are in this verse. The *x* and *z* are not.)

Letter Focus

Ii, Nn, Vv

NOTE:
Directions must be used as part of the Weekly Lesson Format. See page 6.

Lesson 27

TIP OF THE WEEK
The overstroke is easy to identify in letters like *n* and *m*. Watch for other overstroke letters as you practice this week. (Hint: Four are in this verse, and two are not.)

Day One   Practice the following letters and words from this week's Scripture.

Ii

conceited

will

health

Day Two   Continue practicing letters and words from this week's Scripture.

Nn

turn

renewed

given

61

Copyright©2001 by Concerned Communications. All rights reserved.

✏ Extended Teaching

● Ask your students to define the word *vitality* (exuberant physical and mental strength; capacity for survival or endurance; power to live or grow).

● Have students rewrite the verse using words from the definition to better understand the verse. (example: ". . .you will be given renewed health and exuberant physical and mental strength.")

✏ For Discussion

"Proverbs 16:18 offers additional insight into this topic. Describe its similarities to this week's verse." (Pride, conceit, and haughtiness are similar traits that detract from a healthy body and mind. For discussion: "When we fall down, the only direction to look is up!")

Day Three   Continue practicing letters and words from this week's Scripture.

Vv

evil

reverence

vitality

Day Four   Write this week's Scripture verse on a sheet of practice paper.

Don't be conceited, sure of your own wisdom. Instead, trust and reverence the Lord, and turn your back on evil; when you do that, then you will be given renewed health and vitality.

Proverbs 3:7,8

FOR DISCUSSION
Proverbs 16:18 offers additional insight into this topic. Describe its similarities to this week's verse.

62

Copyright©2001 by Concerned Communications. All rights reserved.

Scripture Verse

"We can justify our every deed but God looks at our motives. God is more pleased when we are just and fair than when we give Him gifts." Proverbs 21:2, 3

Tip of the Week

"This verse contains the lowercase tail letters: *f, g, j, p,* and *y*. As you write, make certain that you extend all these letters to the lower line."

Letter Focus

Ww, Jj, Mm

NOTE:
Directions must be used as part of the Weekly Lesson Format. See page 6.

TIP OF THE WEEK
This verse contains the lowercase tail letters *f, g, j, p,* and *y*. As you write, make certain that you extend all these letters to the lower line.

Lesson 28

Day One   Practice the following letters and words from this week's Scripture.

W w

We

pleased

gifts

Day Two   Continue practicing letters and words from this week's Scripture.

Jj

justify

just

fair

63

Copyright©2001 by Concerned Communications. All rights reserved.

Extended Teaching

• The words *justify* and *exit* each contain three two-stroke letters. Remind students that the second stroke is added after the word is written.

• This week, have your students practice the verse once in manuscript, and once in cursive. Remember, manuscript handwriting is a life skill!

For Discussion

"Can a person do something good for the wrong reasons? (being good just to impress or get a reward) Why do our motives matter, anyway?" (Answers will vary. For discussion: Read I Samuel 16:7 to see what God says about this topic.)

Day Three Continue practicing letters and words from this week's Scripture.

Mm

motives

Him

more

Day Four Write this week's Scripture verse on a sheet of practice paper.

We can justify our every deed but God looks at our motives. God is more pleased when we are just and fair than when we give Him gifts.
Proverbs 21:2,3

For Discussion
Can a person do something good for the wrong reasons? Why do our motives matter, anyway?

64

Copyright©2001 by Concerned Communications. All rights reserved.

Lesson 29

Scripture Verse

"Follow My advice. . .always keep it in mind and stick to it. Obey Me and live! Guard My words as your most precious possession." Proverbs 7:1, 2

Tip of the Week

"As you near the end of this year of handwriting, don't forget the importance of good posture! Your posture has a direct impact on the consistency of letter and word slant."

Letter Focus

Ff, Oo, Uu

NOTE:

Directions must be used as part of the Weekly Lesson Format. See page 6.

Lesson 29

TIP OF THE WEEK

As you near the end of this year of handwriting, don't forget the importance of good posture! Your posture has a direct impact on the consistency of letter and word slant.

Day One Practice the following letters and words from this week's Scripture.

Ff
Follow

keep

advice

Day Two Continue practicing letters and words from this week's Scripture.

Oo
Obey

possession

words

65

Copyright©2001 by Concerned Communications. All rights reserved.

✏ Extended Teaching

• Show students the double letters *ee*, *ll*, and *ss* in this verse. Encourage students to keep these letters consistent in slant.

• This week's verse also contains several types of punctuation. Review the use and purpose of ellipses (to show words are omitted), as well as the exclamation mark, the semicolon, and the colon.

✏ For Discussion

"Name some specific advice from God that you can put into practice this week." (honor your father and mother; don't put other gods before me; love your neighbor as yourself; etc. Phillipians 4:6, Romans 12:9, 10, 11.) "In what way can we guard God's Word?" (show it respect; take it seriously; protect its reputation by living in harmony with it; etc.)

Day Three Continue practicing letters and words from this week's Scripture.

Uu

Guard

precious

live

Day Four Write this week's Scripture verse on a sheet of practice paper.

Follow My advice...always keep it in mind and stick to it. Obey Me and live! Guard My words as your most precious possession.

Proverbs 7:1, 2

FOR DISCUSSION
Name some specific advice from God that you can put into practice this week. In what way can we guard God's Word?

66

Copyright©2001 by Concerned Communications. All rights reserved.

Lesson 30

✏ Scripture Verse

"Look straight ahead; don't even turn your head to look. Watch your step. Stick to the path and be safe. Don't sidetrack; pull back your foot from danger." Proverbs 4:25, 27

✏ Tip of the Week

"Poor handwriting can cause some letters to be mistaken for others. This week our focus is on the h and k. Other letters easily mistaken for each other include e-i, a-o, m-n, and y-z."

✏ Letter Focus

Ll, Kk, Aa

NOTE:
Directions must be used as part of the Weekly Lesson Format. See page 6.

Lesson 30

TIP OF THE WEEK
Poor handwriting can cause some letters to be mistaken for others. This week our focus is on the h and k. Other letters easily mistaken for each other include e-i, a-o, m-n, and y-z.

Day One Practice the following letters and words from this week's Scripture.

Ll
Look

pull

safe

Day Two Continue practicing letters and words from this week's Scripture.

Kk
back

sidetrack

path

67

Copyright©2001 by Concerned Communications. All rights reserved.

✏ Extended Teaching

• Students needing help with easy-to-mistake letters may practice the following words: *hike, hymn, Bible, share, zephyr,* and *yoke*.

• Remind students that the capital *L* is written with a downstroke. Tell them to watch for a similar stroke in the capital *D*. This suggestion is especially helpful for visual learners.

✏ For Discussion

"List some common things that might distract us from looking straight ahead and following God's path." (TV, video games, bad eating habits, poor choice of friends, etc.) "How can we deal with these distractions. Be specific." (Answers will vary)

Day Three Continue practicing letters and words from this week's Scripture.

A a

ahead

straight

Watch

Day Four Write this week's Scripture verse on a sheet of practice paper.

Look straight ahead; don't even turn your head to look. Watch your step. Stick to the path and be safe. Don't sidetrack; pull back your foot from danger.

Proverbs 4:25, 27

FOR DISCUSSION
List some common things that might distract us from looking straight ahead and following God's path. How can we deal with these distractions? Be specific.

65

Copyright©2001 by Concerned Communications. All rights reserved.

Scripture Verse

"I would have you learn this great fact: that a life of doing right is the wisest life there is. If you live that kind of life, you'll not limp or stumble as you run." Proverbs 4:11, 12

Tip of the Week

"Remember, your name is the most important word you write. It should always be clear and legible. (Someday when you're famous, we want to be able to read your signature!)"

Letter Focus

Ii, Mm, Dd

NOTE:
Directions must be used as part of the Weekly Lesson Format. See page 6.

Lesson 31

TIP OF THE WEEK
Remember, your name is the most important word you write. It should always be clear and legible. (Someday when you're famous, we want to be able to read your signature!)

Day One Practice the following letters and words from this week's Scripture.

Ii

wisest

life

you'll

Day Two Continue practicing letters and words from this week's Scripture.

Mm

limp

stumble

run

69

Copyright©2001 by Concerned Communications. All rights reserved.

Extended Teaching

• Show students the signatures at the bottom of the "Declaration of Independence"—especially John Hancock's. (You can find a copy in most encyclopedias.) Discuss the historical difference these signatures made.

• Have the class write a "statement of purpose." (Example: "We each agree to pick up three pieces of trash a day.") Have every student sign this document, then post it.

For Discussion

"List some attributes of right living." (happier, healthier, etc.) "Name at least two good habits that you'd like to develop before next school year." (Answers will vary. Suggest reading I Corinthians 13:4-7.)

Day Three Continue practicing letters and words from this week's Scripture.

Dd

would

doing

fact

Day Four Write this week's Scripture verse on a sheet of practice paper.

I would have you learn this great fact: that a life of doing right is the wisest life there is. If you live that kind of life, you'll not limp or stumble as you run.
Proverbs 4:11,12

FOR DISCUSSION
List some attributes of right living. Name at least two good habits that you'd like to develop before next school year.

70

Copyright©2001 by Concerned Communications. All rights reserved.

Lesson 32

NOTE:
Directions must be used as part of the Weekly Lesson Format. See page 6.

Scripture Verse

"When a man is trying to please God, God makes even his worst enemies to be at peace with him." Proverbs 16:7

Letter Focus

Ww, Gg, Ee

Tip of the Week

"This final handwriting lesson is a good time to use the **Five Star** evaluation once more. Compare your writing from the beginning of the year with your writing today. Evaluate your progress." (Show each student his/her handwriting sample you collected at the beginning of the year.)

Lesson 32

TIP OF THE WEEK

This final handwriting lesson is a good time to use the **Five Star** evaluation once more. Compare your writing from the beginning of the year with your writing today. Evaluate your progress.

Day One Practice the following letters and words from this week's Scripture.

Ww

When

worst

with

Day Two Continue practicing letters and words from this week's Scripture.

Gg

God

trying

please

71

Copyright©2001 by Concerned Communications. All rights reserved.

✏ Extended Teaching

• For a final evaluation, have students write the alphabet (capital and lowercase) as a comparison with earlier handwriting samples.

• If possible have individual evaluation sessions with each student. Focus on the positive areas of growth in their handwriting this year.

✏ For Discussion

Choose two character traits we've discussed this year that you'd like to improve this summer. Don't forget to ask God to help you."

Day Three   Continue practicing letters and words from this week's Scripture.

Ee

enemies

even

peace

Day Four   Write this week's Scripture verse on a sheet of practice paper.

When a man is trying to please God, God makes even his worst enemies to be at peace with him.

Proverbs 16:7

FOR DISCUSSION
Choose two character traits we've discussed this year that you'd like to improve this summer. Don't forget to ask God to help!

72

Copyright©2001 by Concerned Communications. All rights reserved.

Please
Read This
First!

This appendix contains charts, lists, suggested activities, and other tools to enhance the *A Reason For*® **Handwriting** cursive workbooks.

Please note: Except for the Blackline Masters section (see page 85), all material in this Teacher Guidebook is copyright protected and may not be photocopied or duplicated in any form.

Appendix

Vocabulary List

This list is composed of all the practice words from lessons 1-32 in student workbook F.

Aa
about
acts
advice
ahead
always
and
answer
ants
apples
are
army
away
axe

Bb
back
bad
basic
basket
be
begin
better
blessings
bones
born
break
breaking
brings
broken
brother
but
by

Cc
careful
cause
character
cheating
cheerful
child
comes
choose
chooses
common
completely
conceited
control
corrects
cruel

Dd
deed
delights
despise
despises
destroyed
dime
dirty
discouragement
does
doing
don't
dozen

Ee
eating
enemies
enjoyable
enjoys
esteem
even
ever
every
everyone
everything
evil
exhalt
exposed

Ff
face
fact
fair
famous
father
fear
fellow
fight
find
first
flow
follow
fools
foot
for
forever
friend
friends
from
fruit

Gg
gathering
gentle
gifts
given
gives
giving
glad
gloomy
God
godly
God's
gold
good
great
griping
guard

Hh
hands
happy
hard
harmful
harsh
have
health
healthful
heart
held
him
hitting
hold
honor
how

Ii
idles
insist
instructions
is
it

Jj
judgment
just
justify

Kk
keep
keeps
kind
knowing

Ll
lazy
learn
lesson
life
like
limp
listen
live
look
Lord
loving
loyal

Mm
make
man
many
means
medicine
mirror
more
mother
motives
mountain
must

Nn
nagging
need
never
nourished

Oo
obey
once
only
out
own

Pp
path
patient
peace
persuasive
please
pleased
possession
precious
prosperity
proud
Proverbs
pull
punishes
pure
putting

Qq
quarrel
quarreling
quarrels

Rr
rather
really
reflects
renewed
reputation
results
reverence
reward
riches
right
road
run

Ss
safe
satisfaction
satisfying
seems
self-control
sense
sensible
sharp
shooting
shown
sick
sidetrack
silver
slow
slow-tempered
soft
son
soul
speech
spirit
spring
starts
starve
stay
step
stop
straight
stumble
succeed
sword

Tt
take
taught
telling
test
than
the
those

tightly
time
timely
tongue
tree
trouble
true
trust
truth
truthful
trying
turn

Uu
upward
understanding

Vv
vitality

Ww
want
watch
water
ways
we
what
when
whether
who
will
winter
wisdom
wisest
with
within
wonderful
word
words
work
worst
would
wounding
wrong

Yy
you
you'll
your

Zz
Zion

Skills List Index

Skills/letters emphasized in student workbook F may be found in the following lessons.

PRACTICE LETTERS

A
Capital: 1, 9, 19, 30
Lowercase: 1, 9, 13, 19, 30

B
Capital: 7, 8, 17, 25
Lowercase: 7, 8, 9, 17, 18, 25

C
Capital: 4, 13, 16, 23
Lowercase: 4, 13, 16, 23

D
Capital: 2, 18, 26, 31
Lower case: 2, 13, 18, 26, 31

E
Capital: 4, 14, 23, 32
Lowercase: 2, 4, 14, 23, 32

F
Capital: 7, 8, 11, 18, 29
Lowercase: 7, 11, 18, 24, 28, 29

G
Capital: 2, 8, 13, 32
Lowercase: 2, 13, 28, 32

H
Capital: 3, 20, 24
Lowercase: 3, 18, 20, 24, 30

I
Capital: 6, 21, 27, 31
Lowercase: 2, 6, 19, 21, 27, 31

J
Capital: 5, 6, 14, 28
Lowercase: 5, 14, 28

K
Capital: 7, 11, 20, 30
Lowercase: 7, 11, 18, 20, 24, 30

L
Capital: 3, 10, 24, 30
Lowercase: 3, 10, 18, 24, 30

M
Capital: 5, 22, 28, 31
Lowercase: 5, 22, 27, 28, 31

N
Capital: 1, 12, 20, 27
Lowercase: 1, 12, 20, 27

O
Capital: 6, 14, 21, 29
Lowercase: 6, 9, 13, 14, 21, 29

P
Capital: 9, 11, 17, 26
Lowercase: 9, 11, 13, 17, 26, 28

Q
Capital: 6, 13, 21
Lowercase: 6, 13, 21

R
Capital: 4, 12, 17, 24
Lowercase: 4, 12, 17, 24

S
Capital: 8, 15, 22, 25
Lowercase: 8, 15, 22, 25

T
Capital: 3, 8, 10, 19
Lowercase: 3, 8, 10, 18, 19

U
Capital: 1, 15, 22, 29
Lowercase: 1, 15, 22, 29

V
Capital: 9, 15, 27
Lowercase: 9, 15, 27

W
Capital: 2, 16, 28, 32
Lowercase: 2, 9, 16, 28, 32

X
Capital: 8, 19, 26
Lowercase: 8, 19, 26, 27

Y
Capital: 5, 12, 16, 25
Lowercase: 5, 12, 16, 25, 27, 28

Z
Capital: 5, 10, 18, 23
Lowercase: 10, 18, 23, 27

CURSIVE TERMS

CAPITAL GROUPS
Boatstroke (B, F, G, I, S, T)
Canestroke (H, K, M, N, U, V, W, X, Y, Z)
Downstroke (D, L)
Forward oval (B, P, R)
Oval (A, C, E, O)
Tail (J, Y, Z)
Two/Three stroke (F, H, K, T, X)
Upswing (I, J, Q)

LOWERCASE GROUPS
Bridgestroke (b, o, v, w)
Loop (b, e, f, h, k, l)
Oval (a, c, d, g, o, p, q)
Overstroke (m, n, v, x, y, z)
Tail (f, g, j, p, q, y, z)
Tall (b, d, f, h, k, l, t)
Two-stroke (i, j, t, x)
Upstroke (i, j, p, r, s, t, u, w)

GENERAL SKILLS

IN EVERY VERSE
Letter formation
Connecting strokes
Number formation
Sentence structure
Punctuation
Capitalization

LETTER PRACTICE

Capital Letters
Boatstroke: 8
Canestroke: 12, 20
Downstroke: 29
Forward oval: 17
Oval: 13, 19
Tail: 5, 10
Upswing: 6, 15

Lowercase Letters
Bridgestroke: 9
Loop: 11, 24
Oval: 13, 21
Overstroke: 10, 23, 27
Tail: 5, 28
Tall: 18, 30
Two-stroke: 8, 19, 26, 28
Upstroke: 15

FIVE STAR SKILLS
Letter alignment: 3, 25
Letter shape: 2, 5, 13, 24, 26
Letter size: 5, 7, 13, 18, 22
Letter slant: 6, 12, 29
Letter spacing: 22

MECHANICS
Paper position: 11, 24
Pencil position: 14
Posture: 11, 24, 29

OTHER PRACTICE
Combinations
  (qu): 21
  (ex): 26
Connected capitals
  (C, E, Z): 23
  (M, N): 20
  (R): 17
Hyphenated words: 15
Loop/Non-loop
  (i, e): 2
Name focus: 4, 31
Peer evaluation: 20
Self evaluation: 1, 18, 32
Similar cap/lowercase: 10

Letter Formation Charts

Cursive Letter Formation

Aa   Bb   Cc   Dd   Ee
Ff   Gg   Hh   Ii   Jj
Kk   Ll   Mm   Nn   Oo
Pp   Qq   Rr   Ss   Tt
Uu   Vv   Ww   Xx   Yy
Zz   0 1 2 3 4 5 6 7 8 9

✱ This capital letter connects to the rest of the word.

Manuscript Letter Formation

Aa   Bb   Cc   Dd   Ee   Ff
Gg   Hh   Ii   Jj   Kk   Ll
Mm   Nn   Oo   Pp   Qq   Rr
Ss   Tt   Uu   Vv   Ww   Xx
Yy   Zz   0 1 2 3 4 5 6 7 8 9

This information is also available in "Student Alphabet Desk Cards" or "Alphabet Wall Sheets." See your *A Reason For* Handwriting catalog, or call (800) 447-4332.

Extended Activities

As students become more proficient at cursive writing, these activites can be used to expand their opportunities for enjoyable and challenging writing practice.

The Rest of the Story

Some students (especially older, more mature ones) may wish to do further research about the Verse of the Week. Challenge them to be "reporters," and to come up with "the rest of the story." Using a Bible Commentary or other religious reference book, students can quickly discover the author of that particular book of Scripture, and often find interesting background information about the specific verse.

Results of their research may be shared with the class in a short speech—or you may wish to have them produce a written report that summarizes their findings.

The Writing Center

Develop a writing center where students can create "special messages." This activity offers yet another creative outlet for students to continually improve their handwriting. Special messages might include:

- Letters to family members
- Special occasion cards
- Thank-you notes
- Pen-pal messages
- Birthday cards
- Greeting cards
- Invitations
- Posters
- Letters to friends

Encourage students to come up with even more ideas for this activity. You can stock the writing center with items like:

- construction paper
- wallpaper sample books
- yarn or thread
- glue
- bright-colored ribbons
- wrapping paper remnants
- old greeting cards
- scissors
- felt-tip pens
- tape

Include suggested messages, inspirational poems, and additional Scripture verses that students can incorporate into their creations.

Integrated Curriculum

Tie handwriting class into other core curricula. Every student workbook in *A Reason For*® **Handwriting** has a corresponding vocabulary list (page 78) which can be used as a basis for further practice. Ask students to write a sentence using each word from the list. The words may also be used as bonus spelling words or as the basis for a spelling bee.

Other Suggestions

It's amazing how creative students can be when given the chance! Brainstorm with your class about other extended activities they might enjoy. We'd love to hear your creative ideas. (And maybe we'll even include them in a future edition of this Teacher Guidebook!)

Here's our address:

Carol Ann Retzer & Eva Hoshino
c/o Concerned Communications
P.O. Box 1000
Siloam Springs, AR 72761

Letter Group Charts

Many letters in cursive writing use similar patterns in their formation. **Letter Group Charts** help focus attention on these similarities, enhancing the understanding of letter formation. These groupings are also helpful for introducing new letters, and for providing direction in continued practice. (Please note that most letters have features that apply to more than one group.)

The following descriptions help identify similar characteristics of LOWERCASE cursive letters:

Oval letters

a   c   d   g   o   p   q

Upstroke letters

i   j   p   r   s   t   u   w

Loop letters

b   e   f   h   k   l

Tail letters

f   g   j   p   q   y   z

Tall letters

b   d   f   h   k   l   t

Overstroke letters

m   n   v   x   y   z

Bridgestroke letters

b   o   v   w

Two-Stroke letters

i   j   t   x

The following descriptions help identify similar characteristics of CAPITAL cursive letters:

Oval capitals

A   C   E   O

Foward Oval capitals

B   P   R

Boatstroke capitals

B   F   G   L   S   T

Canestroke capitals

H   K   M   N   U   V   W   X   Y

Upswing capitals

I   J   Q

Tail capitals

J   Y   Z

Downstroke capitals

L   D

Two- and Three-stroke capitals

F   H   K   J   X

Please Read This First!

PLEASE PHOTOCOPY!*

The following pages contain Black Line Masters for the *A Reason For*® Handwriting cursive workbooks. Please feel free to photocopy any of these pages for use in your classroom. Here are some suggestions:

Getting Ready To Write! (page 87) makes a great mini-poster for the classroom when copied on bright-colored paper.

Connecting Stroke Practice (page 89) can be handed out as individual copies, or made into an overhead transparency.

Watch Out for These Troublemakers (page 91) shows samples of common mistakes in student handwriting. It can be made into an overhead transparency to help you show students problems to avoid.

Five Star Evaluation Examples (page 93) can be made into an overhead transparency, or copied for individual handouts. This page helps illustrate various points of the *Five Star* grading system (page 7).

Each page of the **Handwriting Evaluation Form** (page 95) makes four copies. Copy the page, then cut these up into individual forms.

*Photocopy privileges extend only to the material in this section, and permission is granted only for those classrooms using **A Reason For**® **Handwriting** cursive Student Workbooks. Any other use of this material is expressly forbidden, and all copyright laws apply.

Black Line Masters

Cursive Handwriting
Getting Ready To Write!

1. Be Comfortable. Clear other books and papers off your desk. Sit well back in the chair with your feet flat on the floor. Your eyes should not be too close to the paper—10 to 15 inches is ideal.

2. Hold your pencil correctly (about 1/2" above the sharpened part).

3. Keep your wrist straight, allowing your arm to move freely.

4. Place your writing paper at an angle. (It should be in line with your writing arm.)

5. Work to make your letters the right size. Remember that all small letters should come to the middle dotted line. Capitals should all be the same size—from the top line to the bottom line.

6. Have a good attitude. Be positive about handwriting.

7. Take enough time to write neatly. Your handwriting makes a statement about you!

8. Practice doing your very best.

Practicing
Connecting Strokes

To strengthen connecting strokes, write each letter in groups of three.

h   hhh

c   ccc

g   ggg

j   jjj

r   rrr

u   uuuu

w   wwww

m   mmm

n   nnn

v   vv

z   zzz

Watch Out for These
Troublemakers

Letter	Problems	Improved Form
a	_a_ _a_ _u_	_a_
b	_b_	_b_
c	_c_ _c_	_c_
d	_d_ _d_	_d_
e	_e_ _e_	_e_
g	_g_ _g_	_g_
h	_h_ _k_	_h_
i	_i_ _i_	_i_
l	_l_ _l_	_l_
m	_m_ _m_	_m_
n	_n_ _n_	_n_
q	_q_ _q_	_q_
r	_r_ _r_	_r_
t	_t_ _t_	_t_
u	_u_	_u_

Five Star
Evaluation Examples

Example 1
Alignment

willing helper

Improved Form

willing helper

Example 2
Slant

half a day

Improved Form

half a day

Example 3
Size

blesses

Improved Form

blesses

Example 4
Shape

succeed

Improved Form

succeed

Example 5
Spacing

was joyful

Improved Form

was joyful

Handwriting Evaluation Form

● Two points possible for each ●

Alignment
Letters stay on the line _____

Slant
Letters have the same slant _____

Size
Capital & lowercase letters
are consistant in size _____

Shape
Letters are shaped correctly
and neatly _____

Spacing
Letters and words are spaced
appropriately _____

TOTAL _____

Handwriting Evaluation Form

● Two points possible for each ●

Alignment
Letters stay on the line _____

Slant
Letters have the same slant _____

Size
Capital & lowercase letters
are consistant in size _____

Shape
Letters are shaped correctly
and neatly _____

Spacing
Letters and words are spaced
appropriately _____

TOTAL _____

Handwriting Evaluation Form

● Two points possible for each ●

Alignment
Letters stay on the line _____

Slant
Letters have the same slant _____

Size
Capital & lowercase letters
are consistant in size _____

Shape
Letters are shaped correctly
and neatly _____

Spacing
Letters and words are spaced
appropriately _____

TOTAL _____

Handwriting Evaluation Form

● Two points possible for each ●

Alignment
Letters stay on the line _____

Slant
Letters have the same slant _____

Size
Capital & lowercase letters
are consistant in size _____

Shape
Letters are shaped correctly
and neatly _____

Spacing
Letters and words are spaced
appropriately _____

TOTAL _____